My Favorite Horses

SHOW HORSES

Stephanie Turnbull

A+

Smart Apple Media

Published by Smart Apple Media,
an imprint of Black Rabbit Books
P.O. Box 3263, Mankato, Minnesota, 56002
www.blackrabbitbooks.com

Designed by Hel James
Edited by Mary-Jane Wilkins

Cataloging-in-Publication Data is available from the Library of Congress

ISBN 978-1-62588-183-0

Photo acknowledgements
l = left, r = right; t = top, b = bottom
title page Tumar/Shutterstock.com; page 3 Nastenok/Shutterstock;
4-5 Tumar/Shutterstock.com; 6-7 Mark William Penny/Shutterstock.
com; 8 Thomas Barrat/Shutterstock.com; 9 Mike Brake/Shutterstock.
com; 10 Edoma/Shutterstock.com; 11 Lenkadan/Shutterstock.com;
12 Diane Garcia/Shutterstock; 13, 14, 15 Margo Harrison/Shutterstock;
16-17 svand/Shutterstock.com; 18 Nick Jay; 19 Robert H. Creigh/both
Shutterstock; 20 Michaelpuche/Shutterstock.com; 21 Marie Appert/
Shutterstock; 22 Abramova Kseniya; 23t Jari Hindström, c filmfoto,
b Jeff Banke/all Shutterstock
Cover Mike Brake/Shutterstock

Printed in the United States of America, at Corporate Graphics
in North Mankato, Minnesota.

DAD0055a
092015
9 8 7 6 5 4 3 2

Contents

What are Show Horses?

Show horses take part in all kinds of competitions and events.

They can be any breed, size, or color, as long as they are graceful, healthy, and perfectly behaved.

A show horse is trained to walk calmly and not fuss or fidget.

Show Time

Horse shows are great fun to watch. Some horses display jumping skills.

Others show how elegantly they can walk, trot, or pull a carriage.

Leaps and Kicks

Some horses perform amazing shows called classical dressage.

They balance on their back legs and do high leaps and kicks. These difficult moves take years to learn.

Many classical dressage horses are grey Lipizzaner stallions like this one.

Daredevil Riders

In some shows, skilled riders stand, jump, balance, and do all kinds of gymnastics on moving horses.

Horses wear a strap with handles for riders to hold.

Sometimes a rider hangs off the horse as it gallops!

A rider may even have two horses and stand with a foot on each.

Cowboy Shows

Western riding shows and rodeos are thrilling! Horses send up clouds of dust as they gallop round obstacles and slide to a stop.

Riders lasso cows, herd them into pens, or even wrestle them to the ground.

13

Bucking Broncos

Broncos are rodeo horses trained to throw off their riders.

A rider climbs on to the bronco in a small pen. A gate opens and the horse bursts out, jumping and kicking as hard as it can.

The rider tries to stay on for eight seconds, using just one hand. Sometimes they manage it… but often they don't!

Fake Fights

Some show horses are actors!

They take part in events retelling stories of famous battles.

They must learn to stay calm around billowing smoke, flapping flags, and the bangs of fake guns.

Charge!

Some horses
carry riders
dressed as
knights
in jousting
events.

Two horses thunder toward one another. Each knight tries to knock the other off his horse with a long pole called a lance.

Horses wear colorful outfits to match their riders.

On Parade

Many show horses walk proudly in parades.

They often pull grand carriages or floats.

Hundreds of horses take part in California's annual Rose Parade.

They aren't nervous near other horses or large crowds of noisy people.

Good Grooming

Owners spend hours grooming
show horses to look glossy and sleek.

Coats are kept neat
with combs and
stiff brushes.

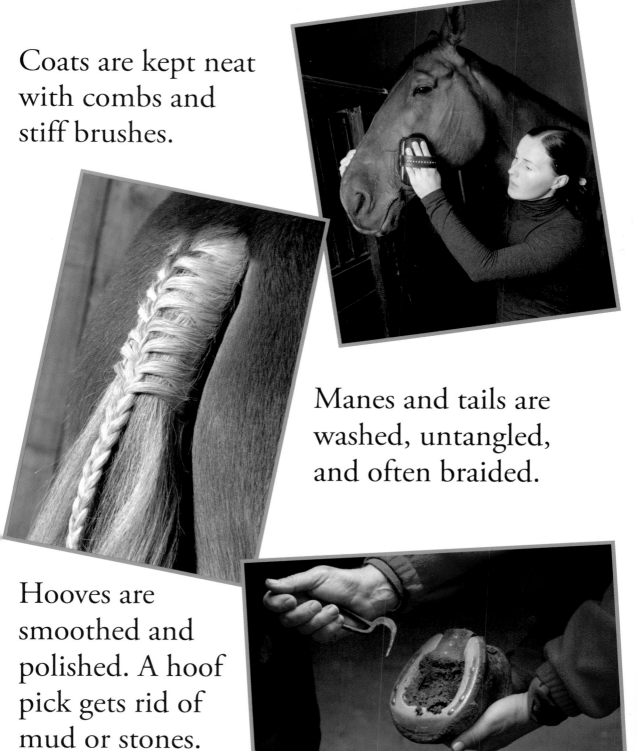

Manes and tails are
washed, untangled,
and often braided.

Hooves are
smoothed and
polished. A hoof
pick gets rid of
mud or stones.

Useful Words

rodeo A competition with exciting western riding events.

stallion A fully grown male horse.

western riding A style of riding begun by cowboys, who rode horses when herding cows. Riders sit on big, comfortable saddles.

Index